THE HEART AS EVER GREEN

THE
HEART
AS
EVER
GREEN

Poems
by Carolyn M. Rodgers

Anchor Press/Doubleday
Garden City, New York
1978

811.5
R

The Anchor Press edition is the first publication of *The Heart As Ever Green*.

Anchor Press edition: 1978

Library of Congress Cataloging in Publication Data
Rodgers, Carolyn M.
  The heart as ever green.
  I. Title.
PS3568.0347H4   811'.5'4
ISBN: 0-385-12795-2
Library of Congress Catalog Card Number 77-72772

CONTENTS

Earth Is Not the World, Nor All Its Beauty   3

Earth Is Not the World, Nor All Its Beauty, Poem II   4

Black Licorice   5

A Brief Synopsis   7

Spawning-to Bring-Forth   9

Contemporary/Psalm   10

Earth Bound   11

Love Ends 11 or Numbers Racket   15

Love   16

Bloodlines   17

Untitled No. 4   18

Blue   19

Towards Spring   20

From Space to Time   23

Convergence   24

Not About Poems   25

Love Ends   26

Paradox   27

Untitled No. 1   28

& Bearers   29

for Lillie   30

Shout   33

Do Tell Faith/The Divine Natural   34

Recollections, Towards a Stream   35

the Joining, Merging & Breaking Up   36

A Round   37

With Malice Toward None   38

Testament   39

Broadway Uptown   40

You   41

rooms are more than   42

City Limits   43

Group Therapy   44

Seeds   45

Feminism   47

"After Such Knowledge, What Forgiveness"   48

The Black Heart As Ever Green   53

Walk Like Freedom   54

Untitled—A Political Contribution   56

The Gary Tyler Poems   57

A Historical Poem   59

Nicodemus   61

For the Others   62

The Quality of Change   63

Overture 67

East of New Haven 68

East and West of New Haven/The Heart, As Evergreen 70

A Reverie & In My Father's House Towards
    Hallelujahs & Freedom 71

living in the shadows 73

Miniature Potters & Significant Clays 74

In Response 76

On Busing 77

Poem No. 1 78

What in the World 79

"Time Ain't Long As It Has Been" 81

Translation 82

THE HEART AS EVER GREEN

Earth Is Not the World, Nor All Its Beauty

Earth Is Not the World, Nor All Its Beauty

the jamaican
woman, a gold
gourd of God &
Africa was singsonging to her tiny
son, "we are going to Jamaica on
an airplane, and aero-plane."
and the little two year old
was resting so lightly on her
knee like a ruby rose petal
singsonging her voice back,
"we are going to Ja-may-ka?
on an aero-plane, an aero-plane?"

some of us come here singing
(it is the "world" that binds our beings)
otherwise,

it is ecstasy to be here
ecstasy
to
be
here.

Earth Is Not the World,
Nor All Its Beauty
Poem II

ah look,
here comes
the forsythia, opening
all golden
like a low down
weeping willow.
the arms not so sorry but
arched slightly, stiffened &
down proud, blooming blooming
all golden and petals belled—
contrasted against stark air
showcased against blue sky
against the blackkneed bronzed Benin
of trees
against the stencil green of April—
ah look,
here comes
the forsythia.

Black Licorice

i have a secret to tell you
i got old, looking at myself young
   i learned how to run standing still
     i gave up, holding on

  i kept waiting for all of my
—this is its—to happen
    and i found out
they had already happened—
    in my head . . .

  nothing happened
i kept on waiting/
   i just keep on waiting
     and trying to trick myself
into not dreaming or
   wanting anymore

   it doesn't work
   i lie to myself
  it's like a religion
  a code of ethics
or a priest's collar, stiff
    around my neck.

or the clamoring in me
   that won't stop
   to tell any/some body
    that
living is life
   and dying is not dead
     we are

often stranded
     waiting
for some thing (some where)
     often dangling
in a between.

at fifteen
pain
called me.
i went to one of the
accounting departments,
the hospital
tallied up
came home
with an appendix in a jar
all swollen, pickled and pinkened

each year after that
i reported in
for some kind of
duty.

by 18,
i had grown something else
with a lot of adjectives
like a notebook,
i was a running account
of cuts and bruises
a writer
you might say . . .

every three years
after 21
i helped somebody
doctors, lawyers and various other kinds of chiefs . . .
the last hospital
sent me home
in a cab

well pilled and still
very much preserved.

i can list so many
scars and abrasions
they make a fine cross
word puzzle
in my consciousness
i tell all my admirers
i'm a different kind of
poet.

i
told Jesus
be allright
if he
changed
my
name.

Spawning-to Bring-Forth

we now know why
the fish swims away
from his place of birth.
we know now why
it fights the rush
of waters as it pressure points
toward some unknown predestined place.
if need be,
we know now
how.

tenacity was my youth
with a certain hull
on the heel of my happiness.
hollow came later
and i yet bloomed like some sunflower in
the open spree of life.
i gathered storms in my fists
and threw them at the sky.
they rained back on me as fruit
which became my dreams
and now, who
not i can speak of dreams anymore
without speaking of wooing.
i woo the dreams that will not
ripen easily, i woo the dreams,
and eyes—yes
i woo the eyes of storms
and people,
with the flute of tears
when there is no laughter
as i wish me some someplace distinctly different
still i bloom right here right here as i am
like some perennial sunflower
the reap of many toils and seasons. and

yesterday
i saw my own becoming—
a diverse disunity/a leavened grace/a silken thirst
a Dahomey thread of
what i have always been.
and i knelt at the foot of
mercy/the well and i cried out to
God.

Earth Bound

Praying primarily and
   fervently in a wind storm
     not to be blown
      away
i glimpsed a black bird
    flying securely and at ease.
      and me underneath me all
wanting only to be blown
     away,
    to drift or ride heartily
    above some cloud
    that would take me
    simply,
    away from all the spit
    of late
    i've seen on the ground.

2.

   yes, spit
and me trying vainly &
  fervently not to step in
the spit (or as a contrast)
    the dog manure gaining grace
     on the sidewalks threatening
to make ballerinas of us all
    (we have a choice/spit or manure)
    in a symphony presentation
    where the music is funky & life and
quite preponderately the droning of
    the possible ineffectuality
     of our own existences.

Love Ends

Love Ends 11   or Numbers Racket

when fingers can move
like hosiery
a slick slide puzzle
and feelings droop
like a sweater swinging
    in my space
some hang testament
then bodies can ball
like spirits boogey
some trial truce of treasuries
for all of us
yes.
it's the heart
that
counts.

Love

there is a light
that comes on
or, is there a light
that goes off.
when you climb up
under the turnstile,
the entrance to
the commuter train
they know. the people
who are in charge know.
out of all the
customers riding the train
they can walk right up to you,
pick you out of the crowd
and tell that you are
the one.
it has something to do with the body,
there is a light
that comes on or,
is there a light that
goes off.

16

move away from him,
she said
and i saw myself becoming
a dim shadow
a silver long elongated acupuncture point
of pain.
who will i be
i cried out to the wilderness inside of me
Yourself, she crooned
                    gently
                        gently.

and i saw myself
turning like a wheel, like a wheel,
the outer ridges
of my rim moving into a new set
of spokes
plucking out each use of dependencies & pain
until i turned & saw him
whole   .
and me, aside him
whole
and now/and then
we were
are us,

together.

Untitled No. 4

1.

when i look at my skin
gleaming in the candlelight
when i look at the full soft curves
in my body/sweeping like
slopes and downs of hills and mountains
when i smell the sweat spice and honey
swelling out of every pore
when i touch the soft coarse wool
cupping the hollows of my cheeks
i turn to the east/i bare my back to the west
i strut across my bedroom windows and stand covered
by the seasons of my loneliness.

2.

it would be a lie to say
i ask nothing of you
for in any miscellaneous moment
i would say nothing and mean everything.
but what have you got
to give? what could i take?
i would snatch your heart and throw it to
the wind and change myself into soft murmuring leaves
that you might so very carelessly kiss.

Blue

what you say
when somebody tell you
he gon leave
and take the threadbare love he brung to your seasons
raggedy love you took & stitched into
the weavings of your reasonings,
feelings you mended & pieced together
and knitted for yourself a life to slip into.
what you say when you find out he gon
make you switch places with his beginning
when he decides to end it all
and the reason ain't clear
cause you really can't hear him
when he don't be saying "i love you."
what you say,
when he gone.

Towards Spring

memories are like dry bones
rattling
in the dark valleys
of our brains.
and sometimes,
images as sharp and as brilliant
as today's fresh snow
flash before us.
cruising through the streets
trying to find spring,
in a random smile or
the careless twinkle of an eye,
i find
the cold is a pout
my people wear on their faces.
no spring today.

but i have memories of you this now
that kindle me
into an amber ember
as i walk through the streets.
like jewels, shining & winking, your eyes
like jewels, your hands & face, moving and still
turn me in the right direction
and i walk away
from the cold,
your face of love
in front of me, guiding me
towards spring.

From Space to Time

From Space to Time

on a day when
we were dark
and not so full of
light
we met
    what did we find?
nothing.
everything, when we closed
our eyes
which anyway
had never been open.

once, we thought we
loved each other
        who can reverse
    time?
we tried.
we stepped out
of space
into some new
step of distance
and fell—
and not in love.

he decided to woo
her.
it was her feet that drew him
in.
tiny, and delicate to his eyes
her feet spoke grace.
first, he told her that
he didn't like the color of her
makeup.
next, he assaulted the way she wore her
hair.
through all of this she smiled.

he asked her for a date.
she agreed.
finally, he told her she would have to get used
to doing the things he liked to do.

she told him only
one thing—
that he talked too much.
he asked her for her hand.

she decided to ennoble this man's advances.
she agreed.

Not About Poems

a lonely poem is nothing
special
   like a lonely person
     you can see them everyday

nobody wants to read a
   lonely poem
like nobody wants to read a
   lonely face
        you see them every day

i can write about love
living high and fine togethers

i can write about mommas, poppas,
show-stoppers & blues
i can write about dreams and
schemes, living & dying
getting down, losing & grooving
i can write about almost anything—

    but a lonely poem ain't got
no audience
  cause it bleeds all over the page
hits and haunts your face
  hurts your heart as much as your eyes (can you hurt)
a lonely poem ain't about poems
  cause it hurts your heart as much as your eyes
    i say,
oh say
    can you hurt?

   who needs me . . .

we competed
for hurts,
measured our
    pain.

like empty spoons,
we filled ourselves
by telling each other
that the door to inner alliances

was our flesh breakings
our façades, falling away.

now,
we huddle together
like mesh.
in the silence that spills between us

the dead ends do not
scream to die.

feeling no pain
he said
and continued to smile
while she told him how
she had cut her heart on the
bladed surface of his glassy high.
as he tasted the grapes
and remarked to himself aloud
how heightened his sensibilities were,
he did not hear her tell him brokenly
how he had smoked the smooth filter of his
cigarette and was holding it as it
yellow curled the edges of his fingertips.
feeling no pain
he mumbled
as she stumbled out the door
that he did not hear close
because he was busy listening listening to
the oarbeat of his hours
slipping slowly, ebbtide away.
he remarked to himself
that he was
feeling
no
pain
no
pain
feeling
no
pain.

Untitled No. 1

the women
clutch
their men.
no grace
to hold them lightly.
tight ain't about tears
but close peace in
close and sure. clutch.
the women
clutch
their men.
their hands caress wise
from children's heads and
mouths that need or leave no
lines to tell
with dish pan duty bound love wounded wiles
their eyes follow
the bias of their days dipped
in search & keep and life itself
clutching and caressing
reason and order
sanctity and peace.

children . . .
any softness would grieve
to call them mouths.
        ache
and yet within all of our softness
there is a core of hardness
that keeps us moving soft to be hard
hard to be soft
soft & hard to keep hands & feet
moving
            to keep young untamed bodies
from aching
        too much
some pain
        to look at them and realize
that someday they will not know
        how/or completely ever understand
            all *"your"* day to day
            all your hour to hour
                    minute to minute
ecstasies or agonies.

for Lillie

who is
a purity.
a devout fragment of
jesus's broken body.
a beatitude of discreet
& discriminating care.
for Lillie,
a sacrament
for other people
she prostrates herself.
sanctified, she wipes
the wounds
stubborn to heal.

Shout

Dee Dee said she wouldn't shout in church
unlessen
the Spirit hit her in such a way
she couldn't
help herself
        (what other way she think it happen)
cause—
shouting
was not her uncool thing.
not necessary
smile, pat yo feet, clap yo hands
and say amen (not too loud, please)
Spirit hit her
it did
knocked her down
sat her upright again
opened her mouth
made a shout come out
and left her sitting
wide-eyes at all the "saints"
who had prayed that one
day
Dee Dee would know what they meant
when they sang
i can't hold it
i can't help it
"feel like fire in my bones"
if 'fen i don't shout
i feel like i might
turn to stone.
even, the rocks
can
cry out.

Do Tell Faith/The Divine Natural

"Hallelujah," the radio minister cried.
"God drowned the Egyptian army in the
Red Sea."

The modern day ecologist, the scientist
shook his head and said with scorn,
"You are wrong. You do err. There was only
one inch of water in the Red Sea at that time in
ancient history."

"Hallelujah!" shouted the radio minister again.
"God drowned the whole Egyptian army in one inch
of water!"

Recollections, Towards a Stream

and when i first
went back to church
i was not there. only a thin
wisp-of-will
stood softly in the corridors
swayed in the pews and clapped
hands and patted feet to the
rhythm of salvation. and everywhere
i went i saw the light leading me,
guiding me home towards some unknown hill
or stream of rest.
now i am quieted.
there is a stillness in me
working its way out towards life.
live, it whispers incessantly to me.

it is the only way to die.

and when she died
we cried
because we were afraid
and yet. too big for
wet beds or clinging
we tightened up.

and when the hands lowered her
into the mud
we were oh
so relieved

for her
for her

let her

lie

in peace.

and we buried our tears
and fears
in the folds of our
stiff
crinoline/dresses

as we fled to the

funereal

of living.

36

A Round

       the long way
is often the
   short way
for me.
     to get where i am going
        i sometimes have to end up
          in circles

With Malice Toward None

when divers sorts of people
want to know about me,
for obvious reasons that is
not love or liking
asking in a manner that is not kind,
    or sincere
i dream of telling each person something different
and arranging for them all to meet
    and letting them be ashamed
by what when they speak of me
they know about themselves.

Testament

child,
in the august of your life
you come barefoot to me
the blisters of events
having worn through to the
soles of your shoes.

it is not the time
this is not the time

there is no such time
to tell you
that some pains ease away
on the ebb & toll of
themselves.
there is no such dream that
can not fail, nor is hope our
only conquest.
we can stand boldly in burdening places (like earth here)
in our blunderings, our bloomings
our palms, flattened upward or pressed,
an unyielding down.

Broadway Uptown

new york
at 3 a.m.
the yellow lamps spot light
the multi-colored faces
and all the sounds.
babies crying, women chattering & laughing
children running, screaming and playing
and men boasting through their dice and drink.
the breaking of the iconoclast/time
to rise/to sleep . . .

these people go on & on, go on
busy with their laughter and their
living
the streets are fluid with the running of
their lives.

somewhere in some huckleberry or
wuthering heights,
people sleep?

You

underneath the veneer of smooth cool—
behind the rose tinted eyeglassed in
glib phrases of "i don't care's" and
"the world should be the way i want
it to be"
there is a person whom i like.
no slick
no cool
no smooth
just, you.

rooms are more than
rooms
houses more than wood & brick
the structure of a heart
is what they consist of
here is my love, there lies my
                              follies

see how i have spread my wisdom
            and sprinkled careful careless
    touches of my dreams

rooms, a house, my home
        windows of a me.

people awe me who can leave
their doors open.
here in this meanness of metal
called city, barometer/chicago . . .

i was bred into straits of
obvious do's and absolute musts
admonitions
braked and braced with
locks and screens.

the southern way was home
long left and gone
not closed but open
running loose with the trust
like a well-greased motor, a
people humming hallelujahs.

coming and going as they pleased
pleasing by leaving an exit as
an opening.
it has to do with the heart, i think
and the propensity to smile to laugh,
or love, or live—
people, who can leave a door open.

Group Therapy

    the bathroom
is a meeting place
    for all of my me's
cigarettes, magazine, pencils, paper,
    we all sit there
    and stare at each other
    and wonder if
anything will come out right.

words are not what people
read
and yet they are.
there are feelings, a symmetry
a complexity of emotions
thoughts, heart communications
and spirit conversations,

that press
through the word
and elevate the bareness of a page

words are not what people are
nor read, nor need . . .
and yet,
they are.

. . . and when we spoke of freedom
        we spoke of our hearts
                as
                        ever green

Feminism

our mothers,
when asked
may speak of us
in terms of our accomplishments.
my daughter is a flower
shedding buds of brown babies.
she holds two diplomas in
her fists as she shows her
obliqueness to a world that
only cares for credentials.
what is your claim to fame?
what is your claim to life—
when there are no diplomas
to be lauded,
no husband to be pillared upon,
no buds to be babied.
when does the wind blow on your face
and in what direction do you turn
when it rains?

"After Such Knowledge, What Forgiveness"

T. S. ELIOT

1.

this morning
this old
way worn woman
came tipping along
her eyes sliding in
on a butterfly
ever so gently
fluttering by
    when i saw
her lips moving
softly/i thought
she might be
singing
but she was talking
to herself as she
walked down the
    street

2.

i thought her
a casualty—
i knew her
a veteran,
of life
hair silver/blond
in the early morning
  light
    this morning
this way

3.

she stopped me
and asked me
if i saw the beautiful Monarch
the royal butterfly
fluttering oh so
gently and majestically
by
yes, i replied
and i smiled
i saw the butterfly.

4.

she stated
her eyes glazed
with breath rolled
stillness in her
her
   voice
     vague yet intense

5.

she told me
as if she were
sharing a secret
about how to make
  fine delicate cookies
    for an afternoon luncheon
how you could catch
  the butterfly with a net

take him home
put him in liquid
chemical
that would kill him
instantly
then take him out
flatten him between
the pages of a book
and frame him/
and look at him/
forever/

6.

she did not
know/did she
what she had said/did she
she said
death
by
destruction
had/she had
been taught to learn
how
the world ends.

The Black Heart As Ever Green

The Black Heart As Ever Green

My heart is
ever green. green
  like a season of emeralds
    green as in tender & like buds or shoots,
        determined to grow
        determined to be
      warmed by summer, winter or any seasons
      sunlight
    green
      like a light
    in the world, for freedom
        for
      what is to come
      what we must know
      what we must be

        for freedom
      for the harvest

        my heart is
                ever green.

she turned to me
and said
the weather's bad, isn't it?
and underneath it all
i heard her saying
i'm white and
we run
the world.

the train can't be late,
he said
i have a business appointment to keep
in only 40 minutes/the train must not be late.
and underneath it all he was
clearly saying
i'm white and i/we
run
the world.

they stand around sometimes
with their faces stolid and impassive
no smiles or frowns
the sum total of often exchanges
just them saying
with/or without words—

we're white
and
we run
the world.

how
do we

dare/we must
go on

we dare to
walk the ways of freedom.

not particularly the women,
but especially the
men.
how do they
run
with those high heeled shoes on?
even when we fly
they catch us.
who needs to be platformed up
to be escalated down & out?
you're down when you can't run
for a bus.
you're out when you can't run
to jump on a train,
for work, for love or for
freedom.
to save your time,
or your skin.

not-particularly-the women,
but
especially
the men.

The Gary Tyler Poems

he was born when the cotton fields first
began to bloom in mississippi & georgia
and other hot places in south america here.
his original name is some word we have
long since forgotten.
no one knows for sure how many times
he has moved or changed his name or face
his cosmetic surgery, the birth of a nation.
it was during the 60's of the 19's that
we first heard of him again.
we knew it was him.
something about his color.
his name then was rap brown.
later on he changed it to huey
and then to stokely
but we knew it was the same him
all the time
something about his color and always
some unlettered crime he was supposed
to have committed.

it had everything to do with color.

now, here/we have
this Gary,
an 18 year old season of injustice
a cycle of congenital genocide
a penal code of get the nigger ethics.
and so,

no wise words for today.
no way
of slapping together profound slogans

that might placate us all in
their "boss" audacity.
this Gary Tyler poem—
it has no end and if you
don't know who he is well
i say "extra extra read all about him"
for what remains
has remained unchanged
what has remained has changed our lives
enough for us to know that
our lives are no different
and yet they are not the same.
for whatever his name, huey
stokely or gary
who will end first and when?
the people,
or the Gary Tyler poems.

A Historical Poem

the world, they say
keeps trying to drown you.
keeps pushing you under
the water, watching you
flail your hands and water
shuffle shuttle your feet
knowing quite well that
you never learned how
to swim
because they did not teach you
made sure you did not, could not learn.

how is it, they ask
that you somehow manage
with all those waves
tides and sharks pushing pressuring
and chasing you

    to keep coming up for air

we pin a medal on you
for this:

        awards, rewards (if you will) of prestigious
    degrees, fancy cars, jobs, positions—

for succeeding.

but frankly, we are suspicious,

that there is something in the water
that keeps pushing you up,

something in the air that keeps pulling you out.
. . . . dot dot dot dot dot

this is how God comes in . . .

Nicodemus

For what is truth?
is the sky blue, if you are color blind
is living a joy if it hurts you to death?
are all men free if they are bound by themselves?
    does pain hurt, if a person likes it?
—the inevitable agony
    of a knowing
that your truth is not necessity
      that all men must speak of or live by or
          with—

where in the patterns of these positions
do men
fit in?

jesus.

For the Others

Since I've found out that you really don't care
and that you like it
when I tell you I don't like
you
and you often want to know
just specifically what it is I don't like
I've also found out that it can
bother me more than it can bother you—
and that you can know me much too well
by me telling you what it is
I dislike about you. therefore,
it is time I think, that
I keep some of that information to myself
That way, you won't know me
the way you might—
and you won't know what
it is I see when I am looking
at you.

The Quality of Change

we have spent the years
talking in profuse & varied
silences to people
who have erected walls for themselves
to hear through.

hearing is an art
the wealthy acquire
or develop for
the poor speak
with the lisp of need.

it is this that
i speak of—
we are still hurting.
we are not free.

to date—
the presidential election
a changing of the guard
while black faces shine as
sweat is our honor/work honest
our ashen hands have dusted the ways
for many white men to ride to white houses
where black faces are expedient and explicable
and fall during storms like rain and pebbles.
presidents and promises are words/synonymous?
no change, status quo the same?
oh say, would you believe,
we are hoping again
for the absence of our oppression
in
the quality of
change.

Overture

Overture

america
the men & women
in the early stages of your youth
the oil seekers, the drifters and dwellers
the men & women who gleaned the smooth
textures of wood, who gathered in
like sheaves, the strong smells of
cedars and pines, maples and oaks and
the loose sift spray of fertile grainy earth . . .
crops & yield
the people who became those things
they loved
crops & yield

now—
the broken things,
whole & wholly

who will love?

you see so many
        graveyards around
these little towns—
        out in the open
            spaces & places.

            i guess big cities
        have not enough space for the
            living,
                    let alone the dead.

there is so much
water here
and back home in
chicago we would call
them rocks, lying all on the ground(s)
lots of rocks around/but
you would call them
stones here.
see how much smoother
the world is.

the farther east we go
go
    the more frequent
are the stops at rich small
quaint towns and the more frequent
are the admonitions to "watch one's
ticket on the rack above the seat
or to be very sure to take it with
you if you leave your seat!"
        apparently,
                the very wealthy,
                        steal.

as i ride the train
watching the many white students
eating out of brown paper
sacks, saving their now
money so that they can
be the very wealthy later
on, also.

East and West of New Haven/
The Heart, As Evergreen

i saw a tree
with its bare branches
lifted up in bunches
shaped like a thousand upraised arms
a thousand upraised arms
like the Jewish candelabra

& in Valparaiso there are trees
all year around that are
ever green
and the grass peeking out from underneath
the snow is
ever green
like our hearts, pulsing towards our freedom,
ever green

A Reverie & In My Father's House Towards Hallelujahs & Freedom

I.

i had a dream once.
only a dream
i saw life running as a stream
a thin trickle
a stream—
a silver penciled line
a crack, a gap between 2 long rocks
i could not see the ends of.
and water silver bright like
mercury rushing, bubbling
trickling and gurgling through—
going someplace.
i saw myself standing by
in front of
on the side of
the left side looking at the right or
the right side looking at the
left
one fish
flat
and me standing by the stream
and the fish
never moving but the stream
moving him her it rushing, gushing along
so silver so silver and the
light the light blind blinking bright
and a house high on the hill
a hill across the stream
and the grass on the hill
not even noticeably green

but more like gray, yes gray & green, damp green
just everything light light bright and
silver and like
            mercury.

2.

was a dream.
and me standing there
calm & dry-eyes
            watching the river the stream and the fish never
moving at all except how the water jolted him, cradled him
and joggled him bounced him
                        i never moved and neither
                        not the Fish
                        was a dream

a reverie &
        in my father's house.
no, not here
but some place very green &
            very different.

tin can alleys
stretch themselves out to gather
the garbage in our hearts.
the refuge is the years
we have spent ourselves
trying to shackle through the
blue mondays, trying to hawk our
paths to where the eagles fly.
the concrete has not yet solidified
our collective citified minds
and behind every wind, there is
a corner that turns into a hello.
it is the hancock way of leaning
into tribunes & towers that nobody
denies, gleam through our yesterdays
& brace up our tomorrows.

Miniature Potters & Significant Clays

life—
it
just happened
to them
just, happened. like
school,
marriage,
illnesses,
babies—
life/it
just happened/to
them
and they were black,
and then they were old & tired and often
incomprehensible.

some people
some
can
make life happen,
to them.
they can make babies,
they can make marriages,
they make debts.

for others,
it just happens.

2.

we want to make impressions.
we want to be significant

                                        parts
              of the cast and not an affectation of it.
                    we want to change
                                        the heritage of the dyes.

we
want
as much good
as we can
get
    here.

their eyes accuse me.
their eyes deny me,
and with their prestigious degrees
from the prestigious schools in pro-gressive
B-L-A-C-K studies pro-grams:

> color ·them successful.
> color them "relevant."

and i, the "militant" gone mild?
well i'm mellow in my meanings, ain't i?
i love my people. i relate to their, welfare.
and even though my picture was in
the hawkeye news-times
  it do not doesn't mean you can now
color me whitened/for i could never be.
  blackness is, it *has* to be
more than skin and picture deep here
    there or where you appear:

> color me

  aside from all of it
      just heah.

On Busing

what de bus gon do
take some chile somewhere where
he kin learn how
he kin learn what
he can learn to
what de school gon do? maybe
Teach, yes

Note: Not an apologia for or against "busing," but a comment on
the concept that the word "yes" is indicative i.e. symbolic of what is
positive, useful—& good in life.

our faces are the
light & dark window panes
we paint our smiles on.
behind them,
we hide the vulnerabilities
we want no one else to see.
the water colors of our tears,
even, the rainbows of our laughter . . .
and the heart that can look
through to another heart
might turn awry from the face,
    but heart to heart
    as face to face should be
are eyes, that need not hide.

What in the World
(a digression)

I.

stop smoking . . .
air pollution.
survival of the fittest
purest of the race s
evolution . . .

this is not a poem.

2.

the last real apartment
i lived in, i loved.
it had a sun parlor
with the most magnificent exposure
for my plants to grow in
& prosper.

prosper.

i was very poor and so,
very fortunate
to get the apartment
because
i was the only
colored they
let in. i used
to sit in the beautiful sun parlor
when i wasn't working,
and stare at the lovely green
plants stretching & growing
in the secret, in the light,
in the dark, a leaf unfolding

every time i/something turned my head . . .
anyhow, after a time
i could not continue to pay
the high rent/the high rent was/
ultimately i decided i needed to move
and how i used to sit out there
in the sun parlor, the sun parlor,
i got broke and had to move/the sun parlor
the hardwood floors honeycomb—throughout
the large airy rooms, but the sun parlor
the sun parlor floor was tile. tile.

3.

and just before i moved/
it was almost one year i
had been sitting out there
meditating and going broke it was one year one day
i stared at the sun parlor floor and realized
that in the tile there was a swastika
etched in every square blocked inch of the
tile on that floor.
moved. i was moved.

no.
this is not a poem.

"Time Ain't Long As It Has Been"

In our church
we don't—always—
be singing
  "when we all
        get
to heaven what
      a day of rejoicing
        that will be"

      because,
    we all figure
      that's true enough

        but we also feel like
            we got—some—
              rejoicing
      we can do right
          down here
          and oft-times
            i feel like
      when we all get to freedom
            what a day of
        rejoicing
        that will be too

          and well
        i say
        oh see

        what with
            bad food
            bad housing
      and
            bad presidents
"time sho ain't long as it has been"

Translation
(thinking of Enoch)
for Black people

The spirits
we are
live like leaves bowing trees
curtsying, breaking & fencing
into winds.
brushing, bruising & mingling
with each other.

I say,
we will live.
no death is a
singular unregenerating
event.
we will continue to be
constant
to flux
into each other
and surmount
the itinerant style of
the incalculable storms.

Carolyn M. Rodgers was born and raised in Chicago, where she now resides. Her poetry has been published in numerous magazines and journals, including *Black World, Ebony, Journal of Black Poetry, The Nation,* and *Essence.* Her previous books of poetry include *Paper Soul, Songs of a Blackbird,* and *How i got ovah,* the last of which was nominated for a National Book Award in 1976. She was a founding member of OBAC (Organization of Black American Culture) and the Gwendolyn Brooks Writing Workshop. Her awards include the first Conrad Kent Rivers Writing Award, a National Endowment for the Arts Award, and the Society of Midland Authors Award.

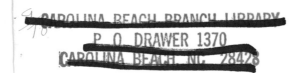